Leaving a Legacy

LEAVING A LEGACY

A unique journaling experience for men to share memories with future generations

By Amy L. Travis

ISBN 9-798986-215198

Printed in the United States of America
Published by FUSION Publishing Group
Butler, Pennsylvania

Email: amy@atravisconsulting.com

WHAT IS A LEGACY?

A legacy isn't something that happens after you're gone. It starts now.

It's not what you leave; it's what you live.

How do YOU want to be remembered?

DEDICATED TO:

Introduction

As you start this journey

Congratulations on taking the first steps toward documenting your legacy for future generations.

You may not remember, or you may not care to share every little detail. Please record as much as you wish, as soon as you can. This is an opportunity for you to shape how your family and friends will remember you for generations to come.

As you complete this journal, consider what questions you wish you would have asked your parents before they died. Know that your family will also have questions they regret not asking. Use this space to respond to the inquiries your children may not know that they have until you're gone.

Finally... this is ALL ABOUT YOU.

To help you organize your thoughts, below are the sections as they appear in the journal:

Your Childhood

- Your birth
- Your parents
- Your siblings
- Adoptive/step family information
- Your aunts, uncles and cousins
- Your teen years
- Your young adult years

Your Family

- Marriage(s)
- Your children

Your Adult Years

- The decades of your life
- Your career
- Your military service (if applicable)
- Your accomplishments

Your Faith

- Your parents' faith
- Your personal faith journey
- Your favorite scriptures
- Leave a message for your children

Your Stories

- About your parents/childhood
- About your adult family
- From work
- From your travels

How do you complete your Leaving a Legacy journal? One page at a time.

Enjoy the journey.

Childhood

Date of journal entry: ____________

Please discuss what you know or remember about your early years in this section.

YOUR BIRTH:

Full name given at birth: ______________________________

Birthdate: ____________________

City, State: ____________________

Location: ____________________

Weight and height (at birth): ____________________

YOUR PARENTS:

Name of birth father: ______________________________

Year he was born: ______________________________

Place where he was born: ______________________________

Favorite memories of your dad:

Favorite memories of your dad (cont.):

What were your dad's parents' names?

What are your favorite memories of your paternal grandparents, if you knew them? Include places they took you, the food they prepared for you, etc.

Favorite memories of your paternal grandparents (cont.):

YOUR PARENTS: (CONTINUED)

Name of birth mother: ______________________________

Year she was born: ___________________________

Place where she was born: ___________________________

Her maiden name: ___________________________

Favorite memories of your mom:

Favorite memories of your mom (cont.):

What were your mom's parents' names?

What are your favorite memories of your maternal grandparents, if you knew them? Include places they took you, the food they prepared for you, etc.

Favorite memories of your maternal grandparents (cont.):

Adoptive/Step Family Information

We understand families can be complicated. If you didn't grow up with your biological parents, please use this space to talk about your family.

If applicable, give as much detail as you can about adoptive or stepparents and bonus families. If you need more space, use the "My Stories" section in the back of this journal:

SIBLINGS:

Names and birthdates (if possible) of your siblings:

Favorite memories of your siblings:

Favorite memories of your siblings (cont.):

Favorite memories of your siblings (cont.):

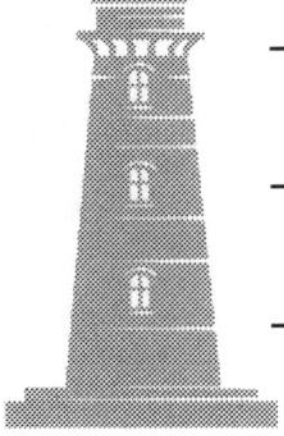

EXTENDED FAMILY

Were you close with any of your aunts or uncles? YES / NO

If so, please talk about your favorite memories of them. Be sure to provide as many details as you can. For example, their names, where they lived, places they took you, and your earliest memories of them.

Favorite memories of your aunts and uncles (cont.):

EXTENDED FAMILY (CONTINUED)

How about your cousins? Do you want to share any memories about them that you would like your children to remember?

Favorite memories of your cousins (cont.):

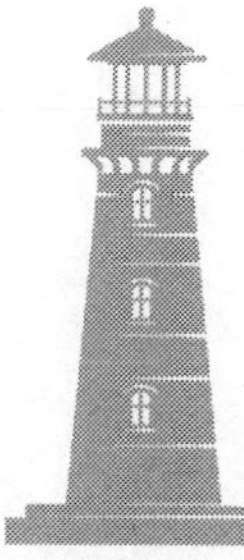

CHILDHOOD HOME(S):

Did you move often? Did you live in the same house all of your childhood? What do you remember about your childhood home(s)? Talk about what you remember about the house(s), neighborhood(s), neighbors, etc.

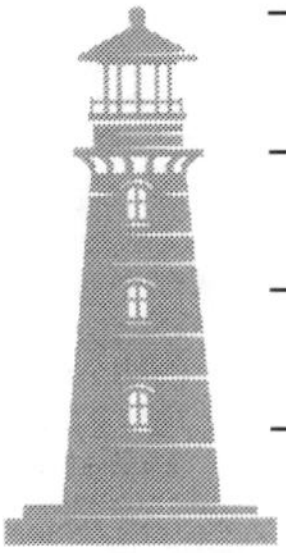

Where did you attend grade school?

Who were your best friends?

What sports/activities or clubs were you involved in?

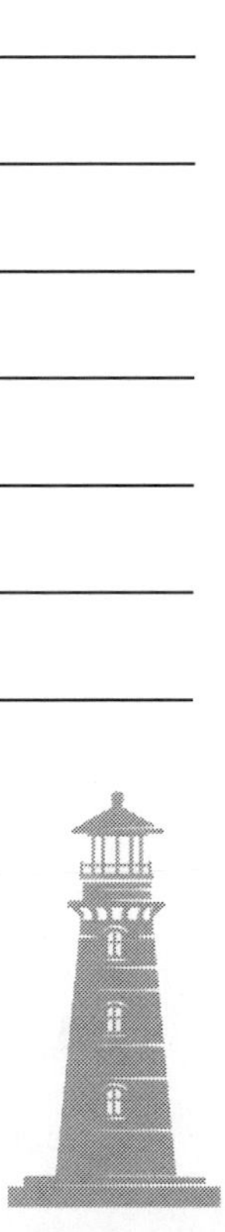

Your childhood (cont.):

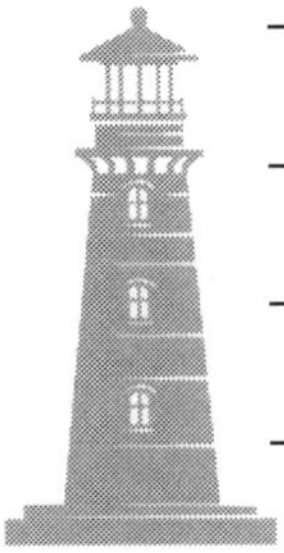

Your childhood (cont.):

If you have more stories to tell, please use
the "My Stories" section at the end of this journal.

Pictures

Pictures

TEENAGE YEARS

Talk about what you remember about this time. Sometimes, your teenage years can be the best time of your life, but often they can be difficult. Talk about this phase of life as much as you would like.

Where did you attend high school?

Who were your best friends?

What sports/activities were you involved in?

What was your favorite subject(s) in high school?

What did you want to be "when you grew up"?

Did you have a job(s) in high school? Where did you work?

What do you remember most about your teenage years?

Favorite memories of your teenage years:

Favorite memories of your teenage years (cont.):

Favorite memories of your teenage years (cont.):

Young Adult Years

Did you attend college following graduation from high school, get married, go into the military, or take a job?

If you went to college, did you learn anything that you still carry with you today?

What was your first job after high school or college? What do you remember about it? Questions about your career will appear in the next section.

Talk about anywhere you traveled or visited during these years.

Pictures

Pictures

Family

YOUR FAMILY

Use this section to talk about the new family you built with your wife.

We understand families can be complicated. There will be space later in this section to elaborate on any bonus families.

I married ____________________ on ______________, _____.

Tell the story about how you met your wife. What attracted you to her at first?

Did you go on a honeymoon? _________ If so, where?

Where did you live when you got married?

Share any other memories of the early years of your marriage.

Talk about the early years of your marriage (cont.):

If you have married more than once, please use this page to share your experiences.

I married ______________________ on ________________, ______.

Tell the story about how you met your wife. What attracted you to her?

Did you go on a honeymoon? _________ If so, where?

____

____

____

Where did you live when you got married?

____

____

____

Share any other memories of the early years of your marriage.

____

____

____

____

____

____

____

____

____

____

____

Please use the "Stories" section if more space is needed.

ALL MY CHILDREN:

Name Birthdate

Where did you live when you were raising your children? Talk about the neighborhoods, your best neighbors, etc.

Neighborhood (cont.):

Funny things your children used to say or do:

Funny things your children used say or do (cont.):

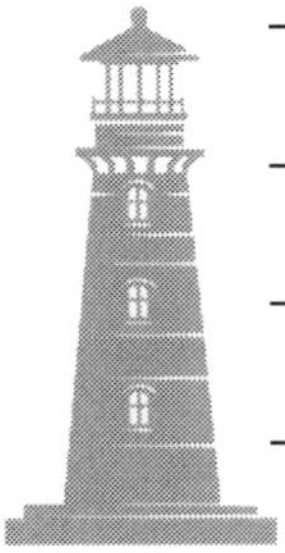

Funny or serious things I used to say to my children:

My best memories of my young family include:

Family

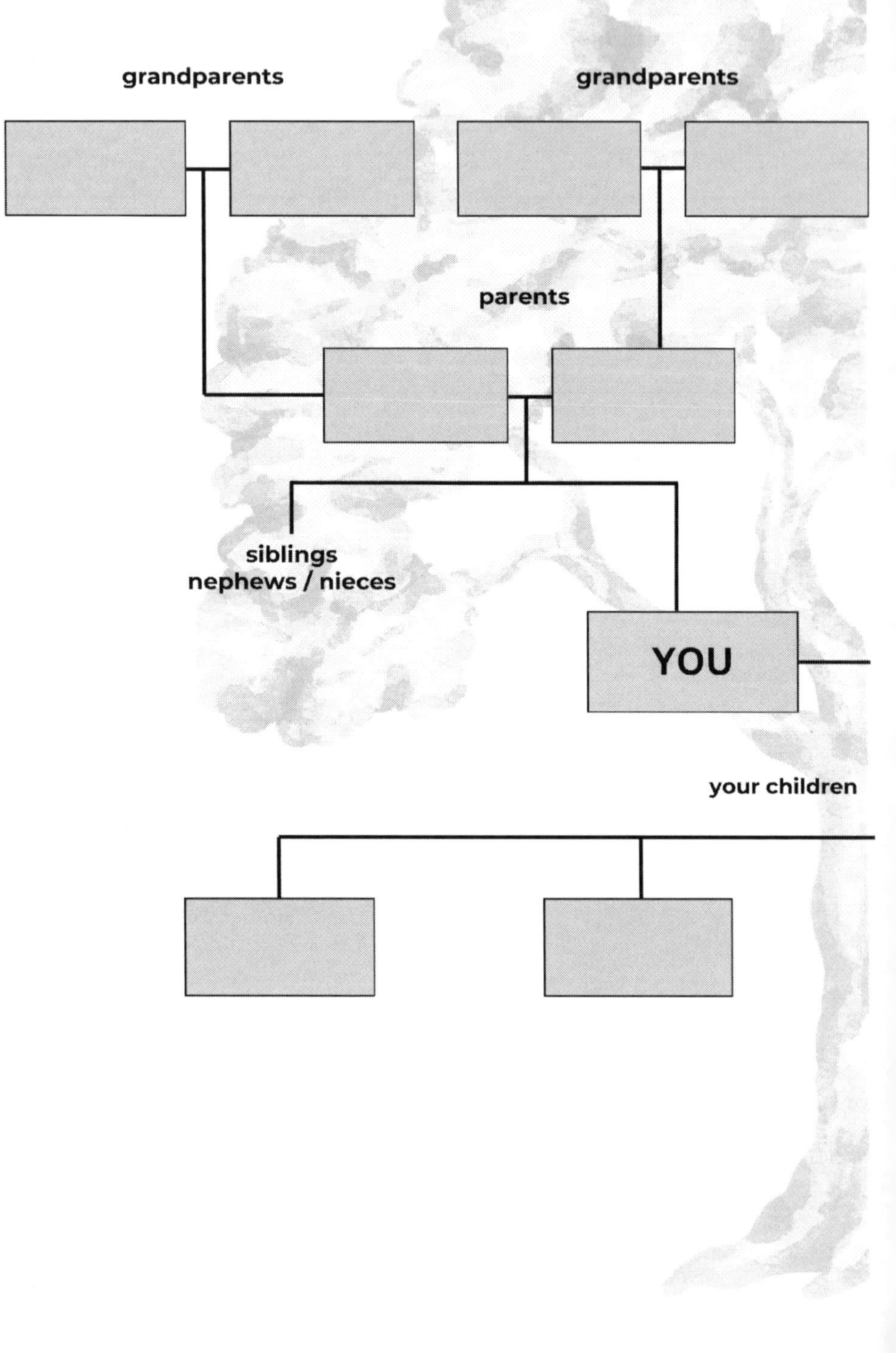
grandparents
grandparents
parents
siblings
nephews / nieces
YOU
your children

Tree

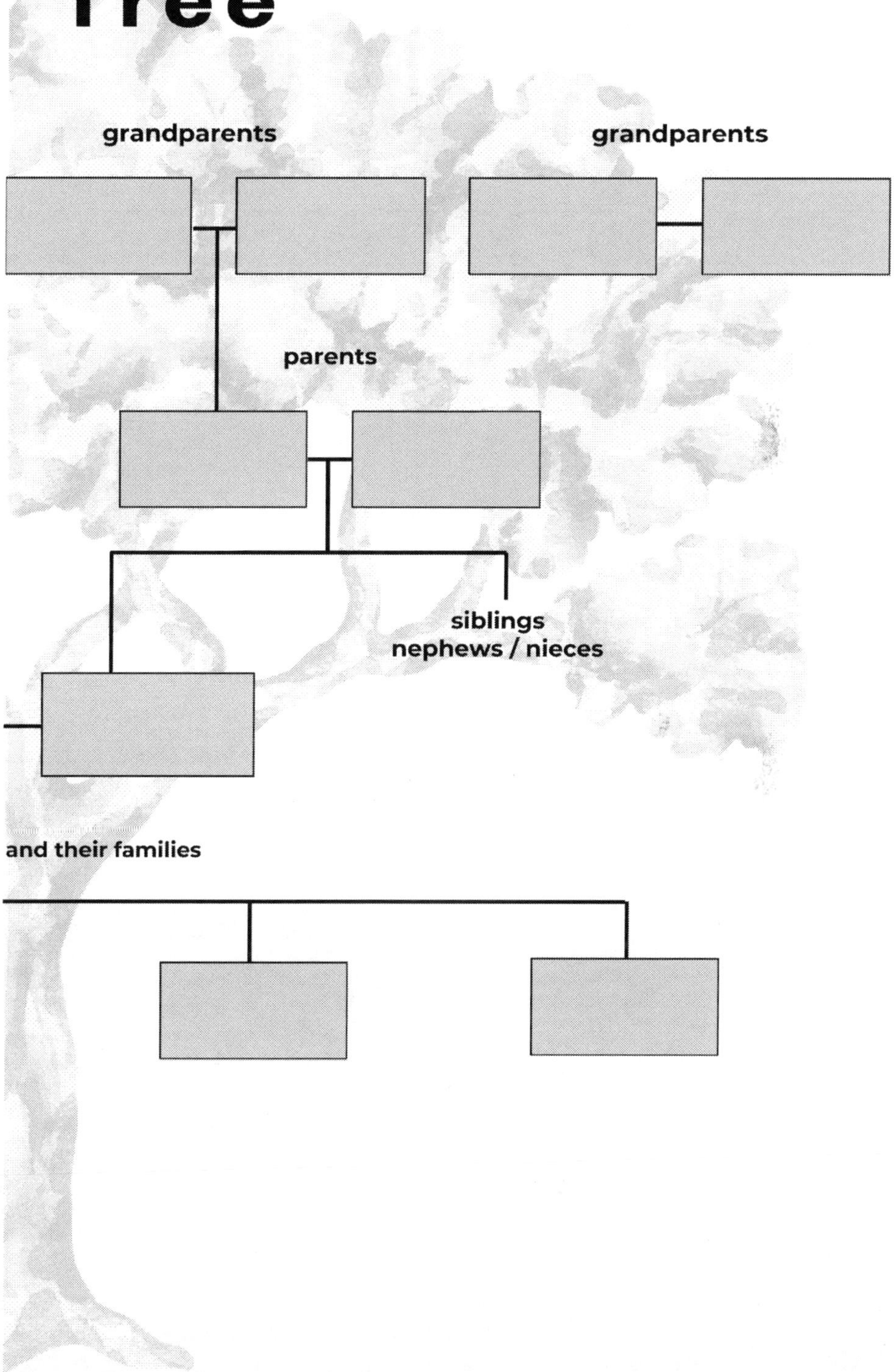
grandparents
grandparents
parents
siblings
nephews / nieces
and their families

But I also remember when…

This may include the not-so-fun times, such as broken bones or minor car accidents, etc.

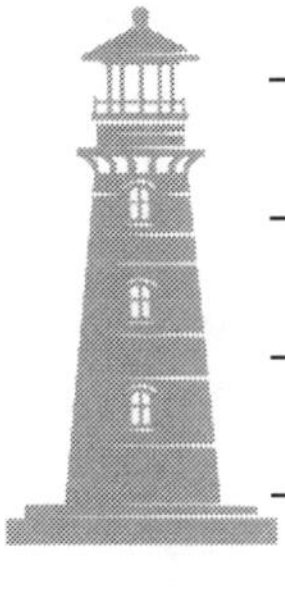

Adult Years

Career(s)

Date of journal entry: ________________

Elaborate on the unique career path you chose. For example:

- Where was your first job?
- Did you go to school for your chosen field(s) or did you fall into it?
- What did you like most about this career field?
- Detail the different jobs you held during your adult years.

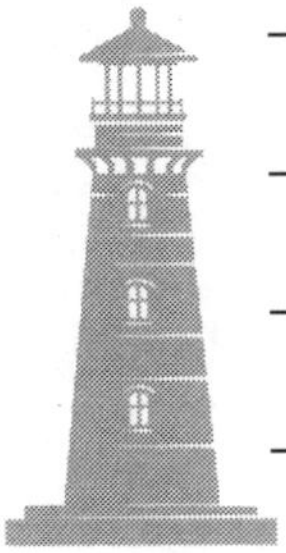

Career path (cont.):

Career path (cont.):

MILITARY CAREER

(If Applicable)

Date of journal entry: ____________________

Which branch or branches?

____

Where did you go to Basic Training?

____

____

Where were you stationed? Please include dates.

____

____

____

____

____

Were you deployed? Please give dates, locations, and as many details as you can.

____

____

____

____

Did you see combat? Although this may be difficult to discuss, please share your memories so your family can honor you for your service to our country.

Military or career (cont.):

Did you receive any awards or commendations?

Thank you for your service!

Date of journal entry: ________________

Paint a picture about the following decades of your life. How did you spend your free time? Who did you hang out with at that time? Where did you travel?

In the next section, we will discuss your accomplishments.

There is room at the end of the section if you wish to discuss more than this space allows.

20s

My best memories from my 20s:

Best memories from my 20s (cont.):

Describe life in America as you remember it while you were in your 20s:

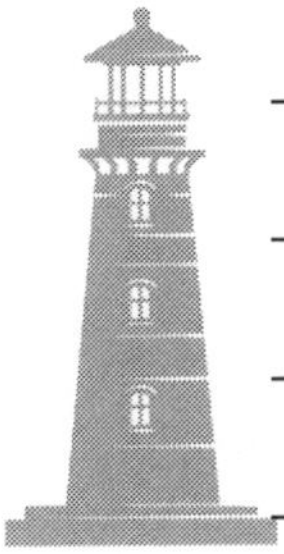

List any events or people who impacted your life during this time.

Date of journal entry: ________________

30s

Talk about your best memories from your 30s:

Best memories from my 30s (cont.):

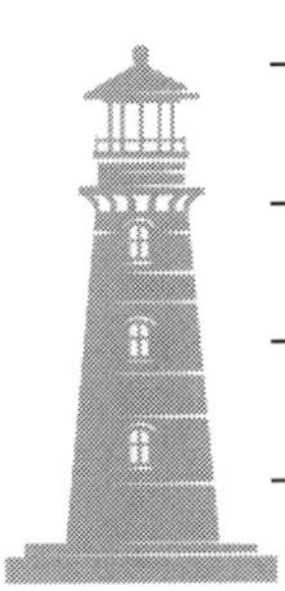

Describe life in America as you remember it while you were in your 30s:

List any events or people who impacted your life during this time:

Date of journal entry: ________________

40s

Talk about your best memories from your 40s:

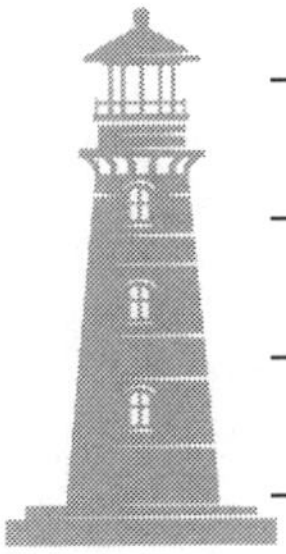

Best memories from my 40s (cont.):

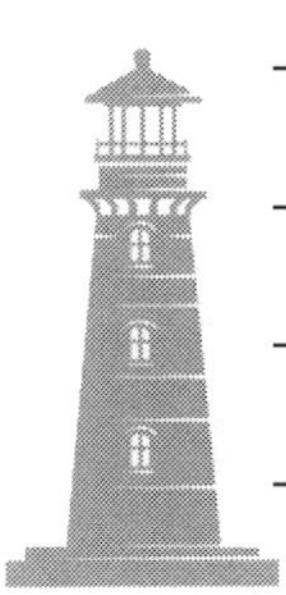

Describe life in America as you remember it while you were in your 40s:

List any events or people who impacted your life during this time:

Date of journal entry: ____________________

50s

Talk about your best memories from your 50s:

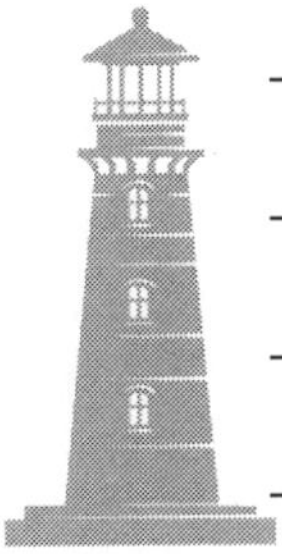

Best memories from my 50s (cont.):

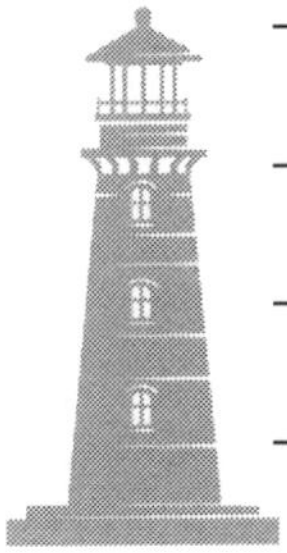

Best memories from my 50s (cont.):

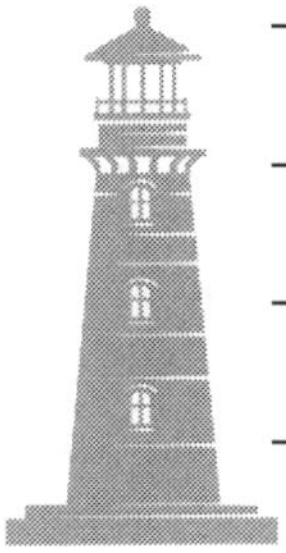

Describe life in America as you remember it while you were in your 50s:

List any events or people who impacted your life during this time:

Date of journal entry: ________________

60s

Talk about your best memories from your 60s:

Best memories from my 60s (cont.):

Best memories from my 60s (cont.):

Describe life in America as you remember it while you were in your 60s:

List any events or people who impacted your life during this time:

Date of journal entry: ________________

70s and Beyond

Talk about your best memories from your 70s until now:

Best memories of your 70s until now (cont.):

Best memories of your 70s up until now (cont.):

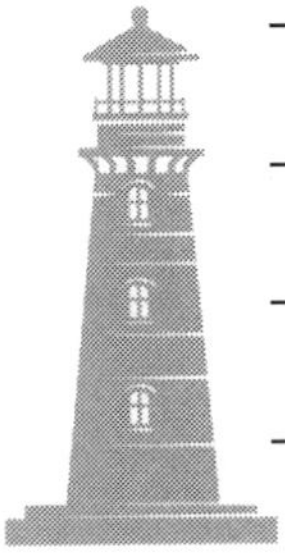

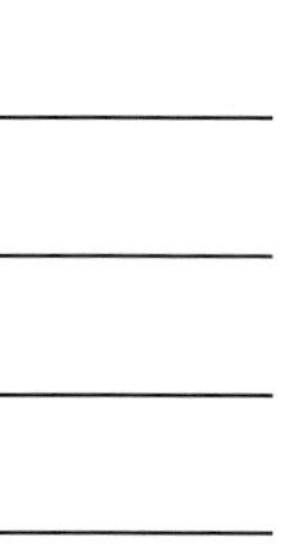

Describe life in America as you understand it now:

List any events or people who impacted your life during this time:

List any events or people who impacted you during this time of your life:

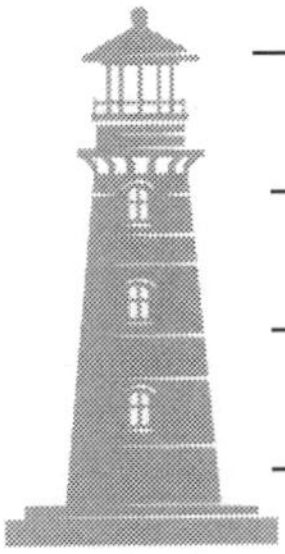

Accomplishments

What do you think are your greatest accomplishments as an adult so far?

Greatest accomplishments (cont.):

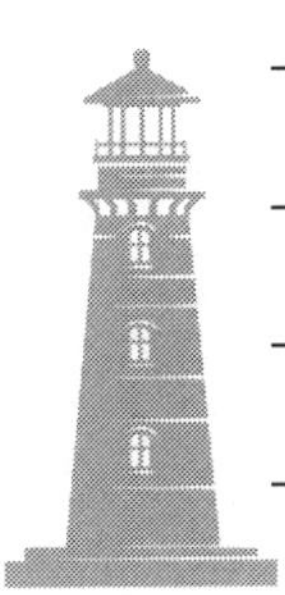

Greatest accomplishments (cont.):

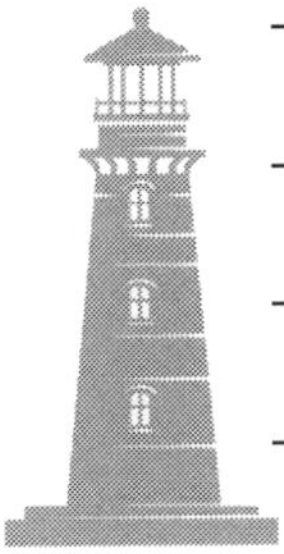

Is there anything you did not receive credit (or enough credit) for that you believe you should have? Now is the time to brag about yourself.

Is there anything you did not receive credit (or enough credit) for that you believe you should have? (Cont.)

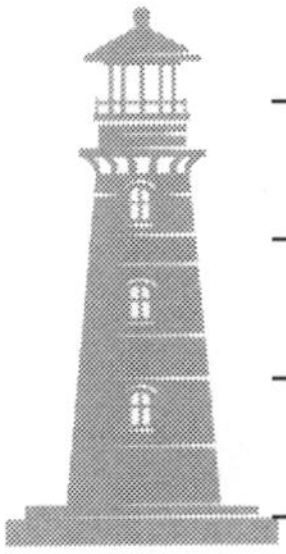

Is there anything you did not receive credit (or enough credit) for that you believe you should have? (Cont.)

Faith

YOUR FAITH JOURNEY

For many adults, faith plays a vital role in life. In this section, please detail your experience and any messages you would like to leave for your family.

Faith IS / IS NOT an important part of my life and legacy (circle one).

If your faith is important, please answer the following questions:

What do you remember about your parents' faith? Did that play a role, either positively or negatively, in your own life?

If and when did you receive Jesus as your Lord and Savior? Provide as much detail as you would like about your testimony.

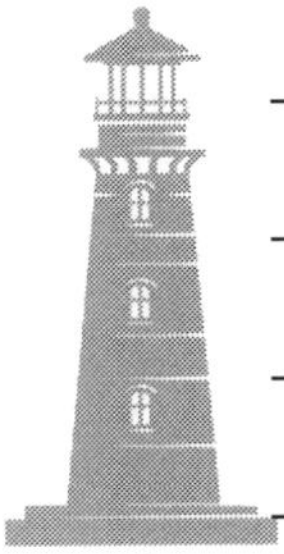

Your testimony (cont.):

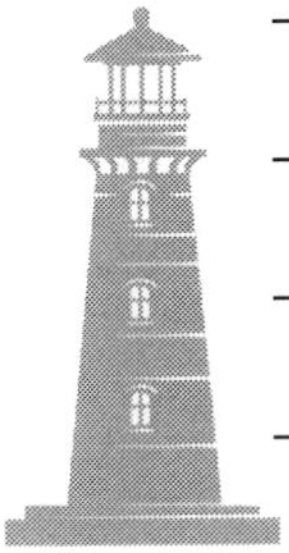

What are your favorite Bible verses, if this applies to you?

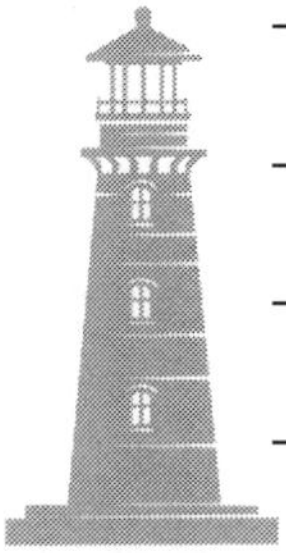

Favorite Bible verses (cont.):

What would you like your children and grandchildren to remember about you regarding your faith?

What would you like your children and grandchildren to remember about you regarding your faith? (Cont.)

What would you like your children and grandchildren to remember about you regarding your faith? (Cont.)

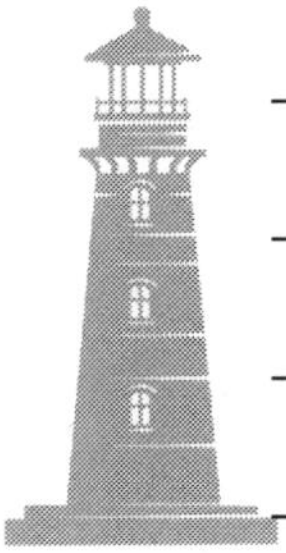

Stories

STORIES

As you reflect on your life, discuss in this section what memories you want to leave for your family.

Types of stories you may want to share:

- Childhood memories
- Unique experiences
- Family traditions

Journal entry date: ____________

Stories (cont.):

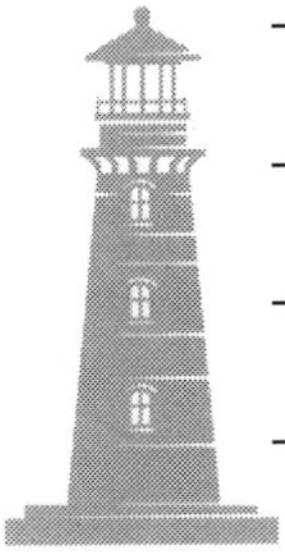

Stories (cont.):

Stories (cont.):

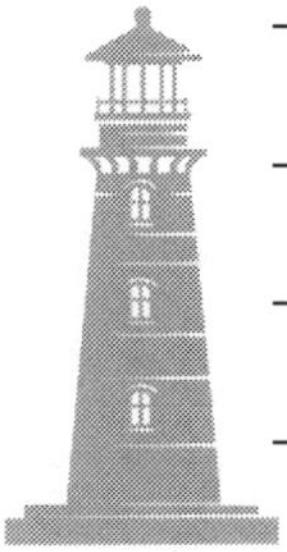

If you find this journal is not sufficient to share your journey, please consider writing a book. A resource for you is *So, You Want to Write a Book?* by Amy L. Travis, coming to Amazon in the winter of 2025.

Feel free to email amy@atravisconsulting.com for more information.

Final Thoughts

What do you want your family to remember MOST about you?

Final thoughts (cont.):

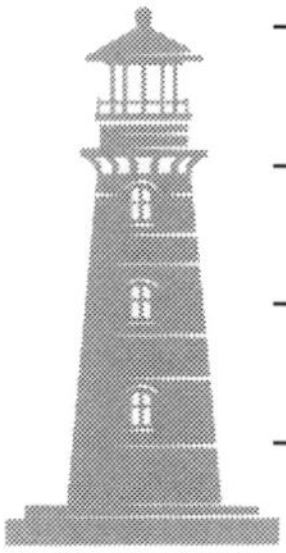

What would you like written on your headstone?

Congratulations!

You have recorded your legacy for future generations.

Signature Date

Made in the USA
Columbia, SC
05 December 2024

6a09a1ea-a70e-40cf-bee3-853b7f244e6eR01